Ethereum

Understanding Ethereum Mining, Investing, Trading, Blockchain Technology and Tokens

Table of Contents:

Contents

Introduction 5

Chapter 1: Introduction to Ethereum 7

Chapter 2: Smart Contracts from Ethereum 16

Chapter 3: Recent Hacking in Ethereum 26

Chapter 4: Ethereum Classic vs Ethereum 29

Chapter 5: What Is Ethereum Proof of Stake 37

Chapter 6: Initial Coin Offerings (ICO) of Ethereum Tokens 41

Chapter 7: Ethereum - Decentralized Application (DAPP) ..48

Chapter 8: Introduction on How to Invest in Ethereum 63

Chapter 9: How to Buy and Store Ethereum 68

Chapter 10: How to Trade Ethereum 76

Chapter 11: The Future of Ethereum 86

Conclusion 90

Copyright 2017 by Harry Lee - All rights reserved.

The following book is reproduced below with the goal of providing information that is as accurate and reliable as possible. Regardless, purchasing this eBook can be seen as consent to the fact that both the publisher and the author of this book are in no way experts on the topics discussed within and that any recommendations or suggestions that are made herein are for entertainment purposes only. Professionals should be consulted as needed prior to undertaking any of the action endorsed herein.

This declaration is deemed fair and valid by both the American Bar Association and the Committee of Publishers Association and is legally binding throughout the United States.

Furthermore, the transmission, duplication or reproduction of any of the following work including specific information will be considered an illegal act irrespective of if it is done electronically or in print. This extends to creating a secondary or tertiary copy of the work or a recorded copy and is only allowed with an express written consent of the Publisher. All additional rights reserved.

The information in the following pages is broadly considered to be a truthful and accurate account of facts and as such any inattention, use or misuse of the information in question by the reader will render any resulting actions solely under their purview. There are no scenarios in which the publisher or the original author of this work can be in any fashion deemed liable for any hardship or damages that may befall them after undertaking information described herein.

Additionally, the information in the following pages is intended only for informational purposes and should thus be thought of as universal. As befitting its nature, it is presented without assurance regarding its prolonged validity or interim quality. Trademarks that are mentioned are done without written consent and can in no way be considered an endorsement from the trademark holder.

ISBN-13: 978-1977762085 ISBN-10: 1977762085

Free Bonus!

Grab your free copy of the cryptocurrency research toolkit.

When I first started off researching for cryptocurrency I did not know where to do my research. Type in the link below to enjoy where I do my own research before investing in any coin.

http://bit.ly/cryptoresearch

Introduction

Congratulations on downloading Ethereum, we hope you will learn a lot from this read. The world is growing, and innovation is what is driving our world into new opportunities. Over the last few years, you must have heard about Cryptocurrencies, and it has had mixed reviews from economists, businesses and even governments. People who are tech savvy have developed the interest in the digital currency, leaving the rest of the world to watch from the sidelines. This book is here to show beginners and even people who have already invested in digital currencies, the current developments and an intermediate understanding of one particular growing digital currency, Ethereum.

Downloading this book will help you to understand Ethereum, how it came about and the distinguishing aspect it has, compared to other cryptos. The book will help you understand the mechanics of Ethereum's operation, which will enable you to approach it with a long-term understanding of where it is headed.

The information you will find in this book will help you take the first step of either investing into Ethereum or even getting interested in trading Ethereum and other cryptos.

At the end of the book, you will learn more about the future of Ethereum, how blockchain technology will grow, and also the improvements that will be made. We are also going to look at the challenges in cybersecurity that plagued this innovation in the last one year. We shall also see how hacking has been managed to ensure the safety of the currency going forward. It is not easy to grasp cryptos all in one go, reading the book several times and getting more information about Ethereum from other books.

There are books that discuss matters on this subject in the market, and we appreciate you choosing this book to learn more on Ethereum. We placed a lot of effort into making this book full of as much information as possible, do enjoy!

Chapter 1: Introduction to Ethereum

To date, Ethereum is the leading blockchain regarding technological advancements since the creation of cryptocurrencies. The head of Ethereum Foundation, Vitalik Buterin, heads the organization that funds the development of Ethereum. Developers from all over the world have been employed by the foundation to develop the platform on a progressive basis. The foundation also benefits from VC funds and teams in various areas of financial technology to produce Ethereum for commercial purposes. In the recent past, there has been a growing momentum in the Ethereum platform, thanks to the public discussion forums, regular meetings in different countries, and even the Ethereum conference that happens once each year. But what brought us to this point? And what is so different about Ethereum from the other cryptocurrencies? In this chapter, we are going to get into the history of this technological innovation.

Did you know that electronic cash is not a new concept? That is true because the first electronic money was tested in the mid-1980's. It was used to promote privacy of transactions, but it failed because of its dependence on central management of information. Decades later, other people tried to bring up new types of electronic cash, but they all failed because of different reasons. For instance, in 1998, an inventor called Wei came up with B-Money which introduced the notion of using mathematical puzzles to create and decentralize money. It was shut down because it could not explain how a consensus would be implemented.

In 2009, Bitcoin, a decentralized e-cash was born. Bitcoin uses cryptography (public key) to show ownership, and an algorithm which kept track of owners (proof of work) was realized. This was the work of Satoshi Nakamoto, who made a breakthrough after solving the two pertinent questions. The first solution was the provision of a method on how the nodes agree on updates done on a distributed ledger. Secondly, it solved the Sybil attack problem, by setting up an incentive for users who participate in the network. This was important because the node's influence in the process of consensus is proportional to the nodes computational power.

Bitcoin's digital cash was later on extended beyond digital currencies. Ethereum took this concept even further by merging the decentralization of transactions, with what is called the Turing-complete contract system. This system was made to help the distributed system of Ethereum to make the process of data verification efficient. To help understand more about how data is communicated between different nodes in the basic format, we are going to briefly look at Merkle Trees.

Merkle Trees

This is a binary tree type that is comprised of a group of nodes that have several leaf nodes at the lower levels of the tree, where data is stored. The Merkle tree allows data that is in a block to be transported. One node can download only one block header from one source, then a small relevant part of a tree is derived from a different source, and the assurance that the data is correct is done. The simple explanation as to why this is working is because hashes (a math process where input data is processed and output is returned as an output with a fixed size) are propagated upwards. If there is a malicious attempt by the user to have a fake transaction during a swap at the bottom level of a Merkle Tree; the change will change the node that is on the upper level, which will, in turn, change the node above, and finally, the tree's root will be changed leading to a hash block. This will lead to a protocol registration which confirms that it is indeed another block.

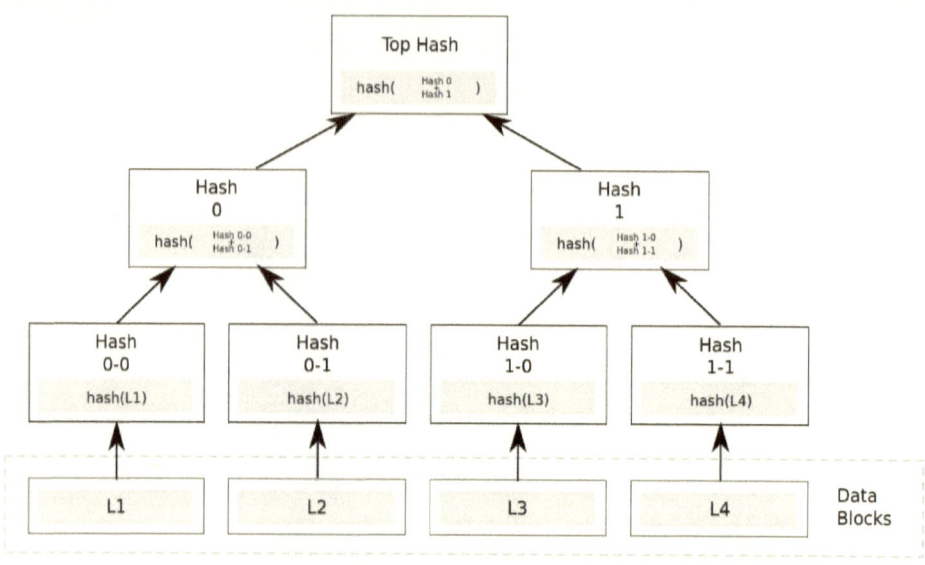

What does Ethereum Do?

Ethereum and Bitcoin are open source blockchains that allow the economic system to produce new systems, complete with the processes to manage accounts and an exchange unit to pass the accounts. The units of exchange in these systems are referred to as tokens, cryptocurrencies or coins, but they are not different from other system tokens; these coins or tokens are only used within a specific system.

Blockchain works just like a mesh network which connects nodes in a network. In case one node of a peer to peer network needs to be accessed via a web browser, special libraries are used, like Web3.js to connect the browser's GUI (front end), to the blockchain (backend), using the API's in JavaScript.

This concept can be used extensively in Ethereum, where financial contracts can be written easily by users in the system; these contracts are what we call smart contracts, which we shall learn more on, in the next chapter.

Parts of Blockchain

A blockchain ideally resembles a distributed database that is used by many computers. The innovation aspect of blockchain is seen when the network reconciles the transactional orders, using just some nodes. The blockchain is a mashup of three technologies:

P2P networking: peer to peer networking which resembles the way BitTorrent network operates. The computers communicate with each other without a central governing body, which nullifies a point of failure.

Asymmetric cryptography: an encrypted message can be sent to specific computers, and anyone has the capacity to take part in the verification process, but only certain recipients will be the ones who can read the message. In Ethereum and Bitcoin, asymmetric cryptography creates credentials for each account, to ensure that the owner is the only one who can transfer coins.

Cryptographic hashing: the generation of fingerprints (small unique pieces of data), allows for data comparison that is secure for any dataset size, which ensures that there is a sure verification process on data that has not been changed. The canonical transaction orders used are recorded in the data structures of the Merkle tree. This data is hashed to become a fingerprint that now compares the computers that can synchronize fast.

These elements combined had an additional pseudonymous distributed consensus which led to the creation of Bitcoin. This combination simulates a decentralized database that is stored in the network's nodes. Bitcoin can be viewed as a virtual machine, but Ethereum adds a trustful messaging system that is already existing in the virtual machine of Bitcoin.

Bitcoin is just part of a large-scale Bitcoin software. Others cryptos include Litecoin, Dogecoin, and etc. Ethereum was designed on a different perspective from the other creations. Instead of looking at the future of cryptocurrency as one large decentralized systems, it will be a decentralized distributed network that enables various cryptographic tokens to be defined quickly and distributed for use.

When you look at Bitcoin and Ethereum, you will realize that, in Bitcoin, certain conditions are allowed to be specified when each transaction is happening. If the conditions are met, a complete transaction is done. When it comes to Ethereum, a Turing programming language is embedded in the system. This means that calculations are done within time and with the right computing power. Additionally, Bitcoin has an average block time that is approximately 10 minutes, while in Ethereum, we are looking at 12 seconds block time. This has been made possible, thanks to the GHOST protocol in Ethereum, which makes confirmation faster.

One thing that makes Ethereum attractive is that in Bitcoin, most of its supply has been mined, and most of it has gone to those who mined earlier. When you look at Ethereum, there is no limit to the supply that people can have. Both these cryptos have different transaction costs. On Ethereum, it is called Gas, which is the transaction cost that relies on its complexity, storage, and bandwidth. On the other hand, Bitcoins transactions are restricted by the size of the block which competes against each other.

Even though there are many comparisons between Bitcoin and Ethereum, we need to acknowledge the fact that they are two distinct projects with different intentions. Bitcoin has become a stable cryptocurrency, and Ethereum has the vision of becoming more than just a currency because ether is just part of the applications in smart contracts. In other words, Ethereum is just a drop in the ocean of smart contracts.

Accounts in Ethereum

There are two types of accounts in Ethereum, *external* and *contract* accounts.

External accounts: are owned externally, and they are privately controlled; these accounts don't have a code, and the creation and sending of transactions can be done by the owner.

Contract accounts: these accounts are controlled by message triggered codes. The contracts can create and send new contracts.

There are several fields that are contained in an Ethereum accounts:

Nonce: this is a counter that makes sure that the transaction is processed once.

Balance: this is the balance of ETH in the account

Code: this is the contract code of the account if any exists.

Storage: this is the storage of the account if one exists.

Chapter 2: Smart Contracts from Ethereum

Ethereum is a practical example of smart contracts. In 2013, it was developed to create a nascent cryptocurrency technology. The reason behind this idea was to build upon the existing concepts, like Bitcoin, then improve the security and transactional speed.

Ethereum launched in June 2015 after an estimated $25 million was raised through crowdfunding in 2014. With its launch, it helped to create a new way in which cryptocurrency technology was being used, even though it was not a cryptocurrency like Bitcoin. Its intention was to create a program in which smart contracts can be built. Through blockchain technology, it is possible to have contracts that self-execute when particular terms or events are completed.

Ethereum is an example of a smart contract that is open source and that is also decentralized. The "ether" is used by Ethereum to prompt peers who have the same network, to verify transactions, achieve consensus on what exists and what has happened, and also make the network safe – this will permit self-execution of the smart contract.

In Ethereum, smart contracts are run in the "Ethereum Virtual Machine" (EVM) which provides a more complete and meaningful coding language than what Bitcoin has for scripting. "Ether" is the native cryptocurrency that blockchain in Ethereum records the transfers.

A token, which can represent any asset, like a bond or house, can be traded using Ethereum, on a blockchain. Such a feat can help reduce the transaction times as well as the administrative costs, to disintermediate a couple of the already available service providers, and online markets that have developed recently.

Benefits of using Ethereum
• Tighter security with every participant, a server, and client at the same time.
The difference between Ethereum and other systems is that Ethereum has several server entities whereas, in other systems, they have a single server entity. This makes them vulnerable to exploitation by hackers and other potential attacks.

Ethereum is also resistant to hackers because it is decentralized, as it has zero downtime, even if there are sections of the system that are low. The integrity of data, when secured, verified and protected, makes the transaction log robust. Altering records is impossible as they can be accessed by anyone in the network, and they are also traceable. There are built-in balances, and checks to make sure that the accuracy of transactions is close to 100%.

• Ethereum is the best way to ensuring applications work properly. When Ethereum is used, with blockchain being the network behind the application, an order is executed, or a transaction is executed on its own, the output(s) are verified on their own, and the value between participants is distributed on its own. This makes it unnecessary to have different blockchains for each application, and also there is no need to have central administration processes used to monitor the processes.

DAO

In June 2016, there were some investors who had issues when they used Ethereum. The investors in DAO (a digital, decentralized autonomous organization), which is a kind of investor-directed venture capital fund, were exploited by hackers who discovered a weakness in the DAO code. One-third of DAO's funds were siphoned and sent to a subsidiary account, which was approximated to be worth $50 million. On 21 May 2016, the DAO's funds on Ether was approximately $50 million which was about 14% of the ether tokens that have been issued until June 2016.

$700 million was wiped off the book value by the hack of the Ethereum economy. The Ethereum Foundation, to instill confidence in the DAO investors and create an opportunity for their investment to be recovered, proposed a change in the underlying Ethereum code rules. The proposal was to have a constitutional amendment to freeze the account where the funds from DAO were being diverted. It was impossible to implement this solution, as it required those who were operating the computers using the distributed network system, to decide if it was possible to accept the changed code. It was determined if a majority of them agreed with the proposed solution, they would go forward with freezing the account.

There was a huge debate about whether the proposal should be adopted and how it would affect Ethereum's principle. In case the proposal was to be implemented, the bedrock Principle of smart contracts running as programmed, without the interference of a third-party, would have been downplayed. On the flip side, if the code was not implemented, the DAO would have collapsed, and the domino effect would have led to the disintegration of the confidence on Ethereum's platform.

The code was adopted in the long run and it made sure that the Ethereum blockchain restored the funds to the primary contract, making sure that the investors never lost their money. It was a controversial step indeed, but it led to a fork in the Ethereum, as the primary un-forked blockchain remained unchanged as Ethereum Classic; Ethereum broke into two different active cryptocurrencies.

This was a great way of testing investors and seeing if they wanted to be part of a decentralized economy, as there is no central authority to dictate sanctions and redress when there are problems that might occur.

Uses of Ethereum Smart contract in Banks.

Banks have had issues in the past with contracts that they form with their clients. Adopting Ethereum in their systems, through the use of smart contracts, can help them a lot. According to an article in the Capgemini Consulting paper in October 2016, it states:

"Smart contracts, enabled by blockchain or distributed ledgers, have been held up as a cure for many of the problems associated with traditional financial contracts, which are simply not geared up for the digital age. Reliance on physical documents leads to delays, inefficiencies and increases exposures to errors and fraud. Financial intermediaries, while providing interoperability for the finance system and reducing risk, create overhead costs for and increase compliance requirements."

The statement above is a testimony of how banks can benefit when they integrate smart contracts into their operations. Some of the benefits include:
• Administrative costs reduce considerably, and
• The burden of monitoring and verifying data is taken away from the banks' hands, and the smart contracts handle this.

The report by Capgemini does anticipate that banks who will be using smart contracts and distributed ledgers have the possibility of going mainstream "early in the 2020s."

Mortgages. Smart contracts could save a lot of money through the reduction of processing costs. The verification process involving all parties could be reduced to sharing access to electronic versions of the verified legal documents between those involved, and the information of the external source, such as title deeds and Land Registry records are accessible as well.

The costs saved are then passed to the client who could benefit immensely from the lending and interest rates, this, in turn, makes owning a home affordable. According to the Capgemini paper, it does estimate that, "consumers could potentially expect savings of $480 to $960 per loan," with banks being able to "cut costs in the range of $3 billion to $11 billion annually," when they lower processing costs in the primary process in the European and US markets.

Clearing settlement. The process of clearing and settlement with smart contracts is streamlined immensely. 40 global banks did try using smart contracts for this, and some are doing individual trial runs. The calculation of trade settlement amounts and managing approvals between parties and transferring funds automatically, when the transaction has been vetted and approved, is done by smart contracts.
An instance would be in 2015 when Depository Trust & Clearing Corporation was able to process more than $1.5 quadrillion worth of securities, which represented $345 million transactions.

Bonds. Complex computation can be done by blockchain, therefore smart contracts can be utilized in setting up and managing "smart bonds." Coding for creating such bonds will be in the permission area, which is, defining detailed rules on who is allowed and not allowed to hold the bond.

KYC. This is an expensive element where you onboard a new client, where each bank creates its own KYC. The result is a high-cost of client acquisition, and the customer will have to undergo a long process of opening a new account if it is at a new bank. One can incorporate this element in the blockchain. Information of the customers can be verified against the center records of blockchain network doing away with a third party.

When a client changes their address, smart contracts make it easy to alter the information, as compared to when administrative issues lead to delays. The coding in the smart contract will notify the clients immediately, and they will resubmit their proof, so that it is acceptable by the bank, without any manual intervention.

Problems with Smart contracts

1. *Inflexibility* – they cannot be easily modified as they are written as software programs. Once a problem arises, it is quite impossible to rectify it as the smart contract transaction needs to be completed before changes are made.

2. *Contractual secrecy* – traditional contractual documents have an NDA section where information shared needs to be kept a secret, but in smart contract, information is available to all parties involved, and an issue of confidentiality is likely to arise.

To resolve this, there are two ways it can be handled:
- Exploring the concept of "zero-knowledge proofs" to separate how verification of a transaction can be done without seeing its contents.
- Information shared through the use of advanced cryptographic structures that only the parties involved know how to access the information.

3. *Legal jurisdiction* – in case of an issue that requires the court or authority to intervene, it is impossible, as it is a decentralized distributed ledger network, meaning that there is no authoritative figure. With it being a new concept, very

few courts are set up to acknowledge the legality of smart contracts.

For this to be a non-issue, the application of a smart contract transaction needs to be correct. Also, using simple terms in the contract would ensure transactions are carried out efficiently and correctly.

Chapter 3: Recent Hacking in Ethereum

CoinDash Hacking

On July 17th, 2017, hackers hijacked CoinDash, an Israeli startup trading platform when it was undergoing its initial coin offering. It was the first ICO breach. The startup was planning to raise its capital by selling Ethereum cryptocurrency. When the ICO was starting, a hacker logged into the site and changed the sending address to a fake one, and it was flagged by the company later on. Millions of dollars were diverted to the hacker's address.

As much as the ICO raised $6.4 million, the hacker managed to steal Ethereum worth $7 million before the company pulled the plug during the ICO. This situation made investors less enthusiastic with ICOs. In ICOs, which is similar to stock market IPOs, the main differences include:
Investors get cryptocurrencies and not equity
Offerings are not regulated.

After the hacking was done, a few hours later, Parity released a report saying that the update was done on the code and the wallet was secure.

$32 million lost in Ethereum hacking

Two days after the CoinDash hacking, three wallets from three companies were hacked, and Ethereum that was worth close to $32 million was stolen. This became the third hacking after the CoinDash hack and hacking that occurred in a South Korean exchange called Bithumb, where Ether that was worth more than $1 million was stolen from accounts of users.

In the same week that the $32 million was stolen, a security alert was issued by a Parity, a smart contract development company, warning people about the Ethereum wallet software vulnerability. Attackers explored the vulnerability to achieve this heist.

White Hackers coming to the rescue

Over $75 million worth of Ethereum was drained to secure locations by white hackers as a way of exploiting the vulnerable wallets to protect the coins from being stolen by black hat hackers. The coins were held by the White Hat Group until the threat was eliminated.

Chapter 4: Ethereum Classic vs Ethereum

In the summer of 2017, when the DAO (Decentralized Autonomous Organization) was hacked, the hackers exploited a loophole in the DAO. However, the ether could not be taken out of the system because the smart contract was set in a way that any invested ether that was subject to a withdrawal was not accessible for 28 days. Therefore, the ether community had time to act, with three plausible solutions: **Do nothing, a soft fork** or **a hard fork.**

Now, we shall not get into the complexities of the two forks. However, when it was agreed upon that subsequent action would be to conduct a hard fork, there was a huge uproar and split amongst the ether community with a small sect being a staunch anti-hard fork. Those who were opposed to the hard fork refused to move to the new blockchain and thus stayed back and remained in the old blockchain and named it, **Ethereum Classic** or ETC.

And with that, we are now in the thick of the ether war between ETH and ETC. The war is not only ideological but also ethical and has been termed as the most important moment in the entire history of cryptocurrency, second only to the birth of Bitcoin.

So, what is Ethereum classic (ETC) then?

As just previously mentioned, ETC is the product child of the resistance of the hard fork and was by virtue of semantics, the original ether. As of the time of the writing of this, one coin stands at 11.35 USD with the market cap estimated at 1.08 billion dollars and it is currently the 5th most expensive cryptocurrency in the world.

But wait, why did some people feel the need to stick to the old blockchain while all the big players, including the founders Gavin Wood and Vitalik Buterin, made the move to the new chain? One simple answer, *philosophy*. When cryptocurrencies were introduced, Ether included, the cryptos were meant to serve one core purpose which would have been to eliminate financial corruption; a system that was not susceptible to human whims. Therefore, to the ETC community, a hard folk would be entirely contrary to what cryptocurrencies stand for, and it would offer a convenient cop-out. By hard forking the system, this entirely meant that it was being altered by human ability.

Then again, what is Ethereum Hard Fork (ETH)?

As already stated, this was a new blockchain that resulted from the hard fork, hence the name Ethereum Hard Fork, and it is considered the new Ethereum. As of the writing of this article, one ETH coin stands at 279.09 USD with the market cap a mind-bending 26 billion dollars and is second most expensive cryptocurrency in the world, after, of course, Bitcoin.

Sadly, however, to the ETC fanatics and sympathizers, ETH is the new Ethereum with all the big hitters moving to it. And unlike what most detractors might think, the new blockchain was formed for one reason, and one reason only; to ensure that the money stolen from the DAO hack was, in fact, returned to its rightful owners. ETH stands for so much more, a victory for the ether community. On the brink of the worst cryptocurrency hack, the community stuck together and came up with a product stronger and better than its predecessor.

Now that we are all on the same page let us take a deeper look at some of their key differences including the pros and cons of either.

Major Setbacks
ETC

Ethereum classic faces one major setback, the lack of backward compatibility. Everyone moved to ETH meaning that ETC cannot access any updates whatsoever that are conducted by ETH. For instance, ETH moved to the new PoS (Proof of Stake) and PoW (Proof of Work) and sadly the ETC community is short chained when it comes to these and other updates.

However, Classic's biggest problem is a conspiracy. A lot of people tend to believe that ETC could be an attempted attack on Ethereum itself. They reasoned out that during the whole attack and split period, anti-Ethereum folk joined the ETC camp just to bring about chaos and disruption amongst the ether community. There have been a lot of references and analogies concerning ETC with a famous financial blogger terming the chain as an insecure orphan child.

ETH

As mentioned before, the main drawback of ETH is that how it was set up goes against its only core value which is to end financial corruption and avoid and possible human interference. Some people felt that the hard fork did exactly that.

Another setback, but in line to hard forks is, the detractors weren't entirely convinced that in future other hard forks were not a possibility. Since ETH can be subjected to hard forks, this would mean that it is entirely within the realms of possibility that other hard forks will occur, causing many different versions of ether and subsequently devaluing the cryptocurrency.

However, this is unlikely to occur since a hard fork requires a majority vote from the community for it actually to occur. Nonetheless, it is also still possible for the community to vote for it and it shouldn't be brushed off as unthinkable.

Let us now look at the Pros and Cons of each.
ETC

Pros
- The currency is immutable and stays true to its philosophy.
- A number of big industry players have of late being backing it hence increased the potential for it to do better.

Cons
- Does not receive updates because it is not backward compatible.
- All the heavy hitters already moved to ETH
- Many people view it as an insult and attack on Ethereum
- Scammers have made their way into the ETC community.

ETH

Pros
- It is growing disruptively and exponentially.
- Constant updates ensure that it works better.
- It has to back from a majority of the original bigwigs and many more are joining in.
- The stolen money was reversed and returned to its rightful owners.
- ETH has a better and higher hash rate than ETC
- Represents what happens when people stick together for a common course. This will be vital and prove key in the event that similar problems and/or new ones arise in the Ethereum community.
- ETH has a powerful corporate backing of around two hundred companies called the Enterprise Ethereum

Alliance (EEA) which include players like Microsoft, Toyota, JP Morgan, ING and many more.

Cons
- It went against its policy core value of immutability.

So, where should your loyalty lie?

To each their own, right? Wrong. What would then be the purpose of this discussion if it lacked a bit of subjectivity and expert advice as to which side of the fence you should be sitting on? Having analyzed the key differences and pros and cons of the two versions of the currency, it is rather obvious which side you should pick in this war. However, being objective, I would urge you to pick a side you feel is in line with what you stand for. Nonetheless, before you hop onto the ETC train by integrity, here are two compelling arguments that you should keep in mind.

Immutability: While we cannot sit and deny that ETH went against policy, the circumstances and situation need to be taken into account. When faced with such a situation, drastic measures have to be deployed. Often, even in our own lives, we are caught out in situations where the solution goes against our values. The hard fork, hard as it was a pill to swallow, did a lot of good for the Ethereum community. The hacker's amount was greatly devalued, and everyone was refunded. So, win-win.

Possibilities of other hard forks in the future: often, people have bashed democracy as a system that is flawed. Well, not in the ether community. This is because it is decentralized and very democratic. This means that major decisions never boil down to one individual or a small group. If such critical decisions have to be made, a majority vote to be considered with the whole community voting. Therefore, the possibility of other hard forks or human whims for that matter is greatly diminished.

Conclusion

Ethereum has faced and beaten the biggest setback any cryptocurrency has faced since their inception. It turned and an absolute disaster on its head and is now flourishing with as many people predicting that it will soon overtake Bitcoin as the largest cryptocurrency in the world. It is also predicted that Ether will also only be the second cryptocurrency to break the 1000 USD mark and with the backing of the EEA, it can only grow.

The future is certainly bright for ETH.

Chapter 5: What Is Ethereum Proof of Stake

If you have not yet heard about PoS, we are going to update you on what is happening in the world of Ethereum. Apparently, Ethereum wants to change the consensus that is in its distribution network to what is now called, proof of stake. We are going to explain what this means, and how it might affect you.

Proof of stake

For us to understand the *proof of stake*, let us look at the *proof of work (PoW)* which is the current system that Ethereum uses. Now, during the transfer of Ethereum, miners solve a puzzle in a blockchain. This blockchain utilizes lots of computational power. Once you form a blockchain, a reward that is in the form of a transaction reward is awarded to you. But it also depends on how fast you can come up with a solution to the puzzle.

When it comes to *proof of stake (POS)*, this whole process will go away because puzzles won't be necessary anymore. The element that needs puzzle solving is removed, and the reward awarding process is altered. Instead of showing people your speed of hash rate calculation, you are required to prove the number of Ethereum that is in your possession. This is done with the help of a master code. When the master code is created, a lockup has to be done on certain amounts of Ethereum to prove ownership, and depending on the proof of stale you own; the rewards will be distributed. You can create several master nodes that have lots of Ethereum in it, and you can earn more in this process.

Since we already have learned the definition of proof of work and proof of stake, we are going to look at the main difference about each concept. It is obvious that PoS is cheaper, efficient and faster. But what is its cost?

The major difference is in the way the methods handle untrusted communication in the network. When it comes to PoW, is a user decides to cheat during block creation, other nodes forgive the dishonest but when it comes to PoS, the user is penalized for being dishonest. Since there is forgiveness in dishonesty when in PoW, there is nothing that restricts dishonesty. But in PoS, everyone makes sure that they are not culpable of dishonesty, to avoid any penalty.

Where do you come in?

Proof of stake as we have seen in other currencies like in dash is an instance where mining does almost 50% of the rewards, and the rest is the proof of stake. Proof of stake is advantageous in many ways. A major benefit is that you don't have to use computational power to solve math problems. Another advantage is the lockup feature. When Ethereum is locked up, scarcity happens which makes the price to rise.

The year 2017 is the year where this project has to be completed, and we hope that the Ethereum development team have to ensure that the code is stable and also provide support to the miners. In case the miners are not supported, then Ethereum will be broken up as it has happened before, something we hope not to see again.

The good thing is that Ethereum has set a strict time for all this to take place. In case the switch is not done, it will all be a complete disaster. We shall see how the progress turns out in the next few months.

As much as the proof of work is going to be eliminated, miners should not worry about what happens to them, because there are many more other cryptos that can be mined. For instance, one can mine a profitable crypto called Zcash when using AMD GPUs. This is an exciting phase for everyone.

POS is not that much of a perfect solution since those who own a lot of ETH have a huge advantage over those who are just learning about it, but it is a great step in the right direction. It is part of the growth curve, and we can only wait and see what happens in the next few years in Ethereum.

Chapter 6: Initial Coin Offerings (ICO) of Ethereum Tokens

Initial Coin Offering? The name might be foreign but I am certain it does ring a bell, does it not? The acronym does sound quite familiar, and that might not be a coincidence. Your guess is as good as right: Initial Coin Offerings are the IPO's of cryptocurrency. ICO is the unregulated means with which new cryptocurrency ventures raise funds. Most startups are adopting ICOs in order to bypass the regulated process of raising capital through banks or venture capitalists. In contrast to IPOs where investors buy a stake in the startup, in ICOs the investors buy into a percentage of the cryptocurrency as early backers. Here, the digital currency, that is usually, new is sold at a discount, or in other words *tokens*. It is usually in the hope that the currency appreciates and succeeds in value in order for the investor to make a profit. However, this heavily relies on speculation, similar to stocks in the public. On the emphasis on decentralizing the currency, the tokens do not by any means confer ownership rights in the respective company. Thus, it does not entitle any sort of cash flows for instance dividends to the token owner.

Digital currency is unequivocally high-risk. Nevertheless, the explosive and exponential growth cryptocurrency value has attracted masses, from professional investors to aficionados to ICOs. Just this year 140 ICOs have led to over $2 billion from the sale of tokens. As a matter of fact, it has been deemed s the new way of raising millions in just a matter of seconds. The wave is causing ripples even at the Silicon Valley from the millions circulating through the crowdfunding. Arguably, this might be a new and exciting business model. To the venture capitalists, this might, in fact, be a legitimate threat that may disrupt their business. Any company that wishes to ICO can easily go ahead and do so, barring any regulatory intervention.

When we look at the turn of the millennium or thereabout, we see a similar trend as we are at the moment. During the internet boom, a plethora of internet companies rose in order to capitalize on the budding and fledgling industry. However, as we know at this particular moment, most of the companies died out and just but the bona fide and resilient saw the light of day. The likes of Amazon, eBay, and Alibaba. In this crypto boom, the trend is once again sprouting. With the ICOs legitimately providing the avenue, the risks involved are worth mentioning. The complexity of the different systems involved the ante on this. Some experts are fretting over the possibility of fraud in this rather unregulated space. If and especially when the ICOs come out on top, and most certainly just a fraction might, there will be some losers. But we are on the winning side, are we not? Ethereum has thus far proven its worth (well not to its full potential, we would otherwise not be here) which is meant to keep scaling high.

Swiftly moving closer home, Ethereum had its first token sale back in 2014. As of 2017, Ethereum leads the ICOs blockchain platform boasting over 50% of the entire market share. Within the last two years, Ethereum has grown and gained astronomically. This could be partly due to the adoption from developers and large enterprise institutions and organizations such as Intel, Microsoft, and Toyota. How so? Well, Ethereum and blockchain, in general, holds the potential to solve efficiency problems in mega scales across the myriad pre-existing industries as well as lead to the creation of entirely new industries. At the heart of this is the Ethereum Virtual Machine. Among its capabilities is allowing a user to create their own token(s). Ethereum developers have standardized this to the ERC-20 that allows for ease and efficiency of interoperability within apps built on Ethereum's public chain.

The Ethereum ICO was first conducted on the 20th of July. It ran for 42 days, up to the 2nd of September in the same year. The total number of tokens that could be supplied was limited to 60 million. In total, the ICO raised a whopping $18.4 million which makes it the 6th highest ICO fund to date. During the ICO the initial price was demarcated at 2000 ETH for 1 BTC that decreased to the final price of 1337 ETH per 1 BTC. The Ethereum team built the system to work with Proof-of-Work blockchain. The blockchain processes circa 25 transactions every second in blocks of different sizes, however, currently the team is underway in developing the necessary technology to shift to a Proof-of-Stake blockchain system. This move will redefine the concepts of mining Ethereum.

A couple of insights have helped skyrocket the Ethereum token to what they are currently. First, the algorithm is open source. The software can be easily and readily accessed by any developer or programmer. It requires no permissions to correct and/or improve the pre-existing code. Thus, collaboration among different industries and companies that are based on Ethereum is improved leading to more efficiency and ultimately better quality of the projects involved. More so, the arguably sophisticated ghost protocol allows it be fast. The standard block time for Ethereum lies at just about 12 seconds. In comparison, it takes about 10 minutes to obtain a Bitcoin block. Smart contracts have also come in handy for the Ethereum Tokens. These exchange mechanisms digitally control and store transactions between the two parties involved. They are usually stored in the blockchain for future execution. These transactions are carried out through Ether, sometimes referred to as gas. Ethereum, furthermore, can and is used for more than monetary transactions. It can be used in multiple applications without necessarily creating different or new platforms. This solves one of the biggest disadvantages to blockchain technology. Additionally, it can as well be created in different programming languages.

An enormous computer network, around the world, jointly manages the transactions occurring between two nodes. This decentralization, working on a peer-to-peer basis and in absence of any central authority, yet under the network's control adds to the systems impregnability. This ensures that the transactions are fraud-proof. Within the system, there are almost zero chances of data loss or tampering. Nil; zilch; none, whatsoever. In other words, security within the blockchain is top notch high. To add icing to the cake, there are absolutely no transaction fees.

The main advantage of this blockchain system is the avoidance of intermediaries, unlike the traditional transactions. You do not need that bank, or the notary nor the lawyer. Since the transactions require no validations, but the network and software, transactions are and should be direct from peer to peer. And let us not forget that with this, the transactions are rendered permissionless. All that is simply required is access to the internet in order to access the network's central node. Could this deal get any better?

Ethereum tokens can essentially represent anything. From a native currency that is used to pay transaction fees such as Golem to as incredible as a physical valuable object such as gold (think Digix). It is often speculated that in the near future, the token may as well be used as a representation of our traditional financial instruments such as bonds and stocks. However, tokens are as well vulnerable to limited supplies, inflation rates, and other financial constraints. Nonetheless, their applicability in various purposes, as well as decentralized governance out, rightly outweigh the reservations. While the functions and properties are entirely subject to their respective intended use, the key fact here goes without saying: Ethereum is a game changer.

There are numerous existing and sprouting Ethereum tokens. The token factory provides a simple user interface that takes you through the process of creating tokens and understanding how they technically work. In order to understand tokens better, you may have a look at:

A) Introduction to Blockchain Token Securities Law Framework
B) The Token Economy
C) Raising Money on a Blockchain with a Token
D) Difference between App Coins and Protocol Tokens
E) The Token Sale Structure.

For purposes of staying abreast with Ethereum Tokens and keeping up with the space, have a look at:

A) Week in Ethereum News
B) The DApp Daily
C) Ethereum Subreddit
D) ICO Alert
E) The Control.

I believe the resources are numerous out there on the web. With these as a basis, you are bound to come across more that will help shed light on this financial path. The crypto wagon has already left the station. But it is not too late to catch it. Jump on the bandwagon. If the promise is anything to go by, the wagon becomes a train. The train becomes an airplane. The airplane is going to fly really fast. And really high.

Chapter 7: Ethereum - Decentralized Application (DAPP)

The life of most developers revolves around learning new languages, platforms, and even frameworks. More interesting is when a developer learns a completely new paradigm. One of the newest and technologically different paradigms is the blockchain decentralized network.

Because it is a completely different paradigm, we are going to look at some technologies that are needed in the consensus network, and also look at what makes the creation of a network.

Main technologies

- Hash Function - Cryptographic

Hash functions take a piece of information and map it to a piece of data of a specific size. For example, a 2MB file that is passed via a hash function produces two hashes of 128 bits size in length. A Cryptographic Hash Function performs the functionality and fulfills 3 major requirements:

☐ No information is provided, depending on the non-reversible hash that was produced by the input data.

- Minor changes in the change of input produce an output hash that is different, in a way that the hash can only be calculated using the hash function.
- An extremely low chance that 2 different inputs can produce the same hash.

Public Key Cryptography

This is an encryption class method that needs two different key creations; the "private key" is only for the owner and the "public key" is used by anyone. There are several attributes that are useful when it comes to key cryptography.

1. The encryption of data by anyone who uses a public key and uses a private key to decrypt it.

2. The private key holder's ability to sign using a private key and the information verified by the user who has a public key, without the uncovering of the information. This is normally used in a DCN's account's systems. It is used to form the fundamentals of transmitting transactions.

P2P Networking

In this network, computers are connected directly to one another without requests being sent to servers. The computers in the network are referred to as peers, and they all have the same standing as the other. This network relies on altruistic nature of the peers, and they share all the resources that are available on the network.

Technologies in Crypto Economy

The Blockchain

It is similar to a database type that is used in a DCN. Information can be held, and rules are set depending on the information update. Essentially, it is updated in blocks that are chained together by the use of hashes that originate from the block content of the previous block. A block has the current and historical information. Requests or Transactions are used to change the database state, and the blockchain stores the signature.

Proof of work

Proof of work was previously a prevention mechanism. In essence, it is a simple way of proving that a large operation has been done. Many times, it is implemented by hash functions (cryptographic). If you are provided with some data part, (e.g., block header and list of transactions), you have to locate the second data part, which after combining it with the first, a hash that has some characteristics (e.g. some zeros that are trailing) is produced.

Technologies in Ethereum

EVM (Ethereum Virtual Machine)

This is an important innovation designed to be used by everyone in a p2p network. The EVM can read/write both executable data and code, participate in the verification of digital signatures and execute code in a manner that is quasi-Turing. When a message is verified using a digital signature, and when the blockchain information assures that it is okay to do so, then the code will be executed.

The Generalized Blockchain and Decentralized Consensus Network

As we said earlier, Ethereum is a p2p network where each peer stores a copy of the database and runs an EVM which maintains and changes the status of the blockchain database. The integration of Proof of Work in the blockchain technology makes new block creation to require the members of the network to take part in the proof of work. Incentivization of the network delivers the consensus for peers to accept the longest blockchain by the distribution of 'ether,' which is a cryptographic token.

After this, we are left with a technology that is not compatible with the p2p or client-server network, because its state is not consistent. Because of the cryptographic security, and its distributed nature, it can be a third party that is not trusted, and it does not have any interference with the outside parties. Cryptocurrency decisions have made the financial impact on organizations, people, and other kinds of software.

This has made developers come up with alternative ways of enabling how different software and components on the internet relate. We are going to use cases and explain the benefits of each decentralized apps.

Development environment setup
Web designers have an easy time designing on Ethereum because the language used in the development is familiar to anyone who knows JavaScript. There are three software parts that each developer downloads

AlethZero

It is a GUI client that has advanced features which includes force mining, private chains, and a full WebKit.

Mist

This is the DApp browser and the mining client used by the client to access DApps.

Mix

It is an integrated development environment that builds and compiles contracts alongside their frontends.

Requirement of the Software

There are three software parts which we have discussed above that need to be downloaded.

The first part is to download is the current AlethZero stable binary, a C++ client, and any operating system. If problems are experienced in the build, then stick to a more current version, which may have fixed the issues.

The second part requires you to install MIX, the integrated development environment for both Mac and Windows. You can also install in Linux.

The final part requires you to install Mist to DApps and tweak the front-ends while you are developing.

Extras

A Mix or a text editor can create the contract code at the backend that we shall be writing. When it comes to serpent, it is best if you set up your editor to save serpent contracts using the suffix '.se' as python, and save '.Sol,' for solidity. Do not use a live refresh when you are working on the front end of the HTML because their testing is not complete.

AlethZero Setup

There is a heavy development that is going on in IDE MIX, and even though there are several features in place, we shall focus mostly on front-end using the client AlethZero development which has a JavaScript console, a compiler, and peeking tools that check into the state of the blockchain.

Our samples are going to be executed on AlethZero's single chain without a connection to the network. Contract development on the test net needs to be reserved for contracts that are going to be shared by others. When alethzero is running in this mode, others may join the chain as long as they are using the same name, and connect directly using the 'connect-to-peer' mode.

The first DApp

We are going to help you build your first contract example, even though a lot of details will be assumed to get to the finished product easily. Let us look at the decentralized web applications.

Basics

The decentralized web which is referred to as 'web3' is enabled by Ethereum. The difference between 'web2' and 'web3' is that Ethereum does not use web servers, and no middleman exists to squander commissions or steal information and there is no DDoS.

A decentralized app has a front end which is written using HTML and the backend which can be referred to as the database.

If you are into the use of bootstrap, you can use the framework because DApp's frontend can access the network fully and CDN's are also accessible. DApp's frontend HTML writing is just like website development and converting to web 3 from web 2 is often insignificant.

If you are a ruby, meteor or angular fan, you will love the reactive programming that is packed in it by the use of callback functions. Another great benefit is that each DApp recognizes the pseudonymous nature of every user, thanks to Ethereum's cryptographic principles to function. In simple words, as a user, you don't have to create an account to get to the DApps, think of it as a default setting.

Installing the client

The most stable version is the master build because the client is not that stable. We are going to use the AlethZero and the C++ implementation for developers. You need to install the master which has the updated features.

You can download the Windows and OSX binaries, and follow specific instructions for Ubuntu that are available on the internet.

AlethZero Overview

After starting AlethZero, you should be able to do something like this:

The interface normally varies dependent on the resolution of your screen.

Now, at the center of the screen, there is the browser which is what we call the WebKit. Browsing can be done from the WebKit; it's just like the normal browser. The other panes have technical information and debugging information. It is useful for the developer and another user. This look is different from 'Mist' which is the Ethereum browser. Once Ethereum is launched, it is going to have a completely different look as shown below.

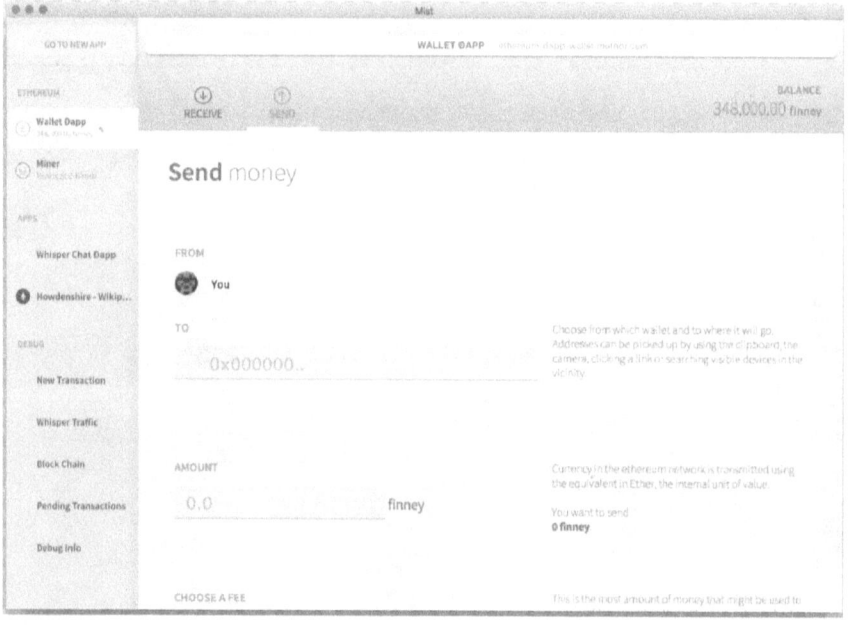

You can reorganize the screen if you wish. Panels can be drag and dropped on each other to form a stack.

Choices

You can build financial applications, games, social networks and even gambling apps on Ethereum because it is a programming platform.

We are going to write a basic contract that functions as a bank, but instead, it has a ledger that is transparent enough to be audited by the whole world. 10,000 tokens will be used, and since it would not be fun to have all tokens to ourselves, a method will have to be created to send out to friends.

This is a simple way of issuing our money. In web2, it would not be possible to have such an app in MySQL and PHP, with users trusting you with the accounts.

Contract

The contract is the backend which uses Solidity language. Other contract languages exist that can be used to build Ethereum's backend, Serpent, and LLL. Solidify will be used because it is the formal language that is supported by ETHDEV.

We are going to do two things to build our small bank.

1.) Create instances of an account that has some tokens for us to start.

2.) to move tokens around, we will build a send function

Let us get to it then.

```
contract metaCoin {
      mapping (address => uint balances
```

```
function metaCoin() {

    balances[msg.sender] = 1000
}
    function sendCoin(address receiver, uint
amount)
Returns (bool sufficient) {

    if (balances[msg.sender] < amount)
    return false;

    balances[msg.sender]-= amount;

    balances[receiver] += amount;

    return true

}
```

Don't worry if you can't understand the code above; It's not as complicated as it looks. Contracts are split into methods. The 1st one is called metaCoin. It's a special constructor that stipulates the initial state of a data storage contract. Constructor functions are named just as the contracts. This code of initialization is run once after the creation of the contract.

The contract code follows suit; it is the part that lives eternally in the Ethereum network. In our instance, it is a function that counter-checks that the sender has a balance large enough which if it is confirmed, a transfer of token is done to another account.

In detail,
`mapping address => uint) balances;`

This code creates a storage mapping where the code can write information to the storage of the contract. In this code, the mapping is defined for important value pairs that are the type address and uint defined as balances. This is the repository of the coin balances. The two data types we have addressed include uint and address.

```
function metaCoin() {
          balances[msg.sender] = 10000;
     }
```

This is the contract initialization which will be run once, and it does several things. One, it looks up public addresses using msg.sender, for the sender of the transaction, which is you in this case. Secondly, it accesses the contracts storage using mapping balances.

Let us look at the 'sendCoin' function that will be executed when the contract is called. It is the only called executable function. There are two arguments in the function, receiver, and amount. The receiver is a 160-bit public address and amount is tokens to be sent to the receiver.

The balance is going to be checked on the first line. If it is less than the tokens being sent, the other code is not executed. If the balance is more than enough, there will be a false conditional evaluation and the amount will be subtracted by the two lines from the balance: `balances[msg.sender]-= amount;`, and the balance of the recipient's account is added. `Balances[receiver] += amount;`.

Now you have a function that sends tokens between accounts.

There are more details that you need to learn about DApp that can be found in more advanced books. You still have to learn about how to contact storage, JavaScript API 1, 2 & 3, contracts which send transactions, variables, contracts interaction, Event Logging, Gas & Gas Price and how to use Mix.

Chapter 8: Introduction on How to Invest in Ethereum

On July 2015, the Ethereum blockchain was born, valued at less than a dollar. By the time March 2017 passed, Ethereum surged in price. We are going to look at how the value grew if it is a good investment and the risks when shopping for Ether.

To understand the value proposition of Ethereum, we need to look at the unique attributes that it offers and why it has a large investor base.

Why Ethereum?

This crypto asset is different from other asses which are backed by gold or the government promises. For us to understand as to whether Ethereum is a good buy, we need to examine the Ethereum blockchain value.

Underlying mathematical concepts

Ethereum blockchain operates under the guidance of the mathematical laws. Its coin distribution is in an immutable code that is available in public and agreed via a consensus. It is the encryption and the mathematics behind it that provide sureties on this asset.

Ethereum is inflationary; five ether coins are added in the system each time the next block that is valid is found. Unlike Bitcoins whose numbers are limited to only 21 million, Ethereum is limitless. On the other side, inflation rate decreases over time as the five ethers become a tiny percentage of the entire supply.

Sovereignty

The Ethereum blockchain transactions are valid because of various factors. The most common of them all is that the balance has to be larger than the sending amount. The purpose with which you are sending the coins is not important.

Efficiency

The cost of Ethereum transactions is low because it is capable of doing 15 transactions in a second. There are upgrades in the protocol that will be happening in the next 12 months to raise the figure too well over 1000. Let's put this into context. VISA normally received over 2,000 transactions in a second.

If you add 3rd party channels of payment that are developed, the transactions will be taken from the Ethereum blockchain without the worry of security or fees. This will increase the network's capacity.

Liquidity

Ethereum is in high demand. Most of the Ethereum exchanges will complete million-dollar transactions in seconds without the price moving. There is going to be a rise in the liquidity, even though we have experienced short flash crashes. However, most users and investors have benefited from Ethereum liquidity due to the fast exchange between fiat currency and Ethereum tokens.

Why Should you invest in Ethereum?

There are several examples as to why Ethereum can be invested in. A couple of examples follow.
- You can access token sales and other investments on blockchain
- You can hedge against fiat currency systems
- It is a great diversification class
- You can use EVM and smart contract if you want to benefit in transactions

- You can also use it to pay salaries internationally.

Ethereum Investment Strategy

Encryption is suitable for different investors because it depends on the risk tolerance of each. Use this guide for information purposes, but consult a financial advisor before making an investment decision.

Buy and Diversify

It has been stated that predicting the future of Ethereum is like predicting how the weather will be like in the next 5 years. Ethereum is here to stay, but just like Ethereum has shown the world, a small crypto set can become dominant in a very short time. Buying Ethereum to exchange crypto assets like Ethereum Classic and Ripple is a way to hedge against the price outcome of coins. It is important to note that some crypto coins will fall, but technologists and other stakeholders have agreed that some crypto asses will become a norm in the near future.

Buy and hold

If Ethereum replaces any form of fiat currency, the value of Ethereum will soar. We can say the same thing if Ethereum becomes the primary currency on web payments that enables billions of devices to transact efficiently.

If you are looking to buy, consider doing dollar cost averaging; total investment amount spent over a period to purchase Ether.

Ethereum Trading

There are investors who prefer to trade crypto assets like in exchanges like GDAX or Poloniex. It is a risky ground on an already volatile asset class, and it should be approached with caution. More on Ethereum trading ahead.

Is it late to purchase Ethereum?

If mobile payments and other web transactions were using Ethereum as the digital currency, then it would be too late to purchase Ethereum. The price of Ethereum will likely be $0.00 or maybe a stable figure once the goal of the currency has been achieved. The currency will fluctuate as an investor jumps on the bandwagon, but for the technology to succeed, the price, in the long run, will have to be higher in the future.

Chapter 9: How to Buy and Store Ethereum

It is not easy for a newbie who has just gotten into the crypto world to know where to purchase and keep Ethereum. It is a confusing process. The good thing is that we are going to help you with this dilemma. Since you have already known more about Ethereum, we are going to explore some other options of where you can buy them

Using Fiat Currency to buy Ethereum

Using fiat currency like USD, GBP or EUR, you can purchase Ethereum directly. You only need either a credit or debit card or a simple bank account to do international transfers.

Register an account on an exchange platform like the ones listed below, verify your identity, add a payment method, and you can purchase your Ether.

The process of verification is quicker, and it is progressively becoming faster, and the purchasing process is getting to be easier. A few years back, the process was extremely tedious when purchasing Ether. For instance, one had to buy Bitcoin first; then an ETH wallet had to be created, then the conversion of BTC to ETH had to be done which was complicated. The cost of all these transactions was high. Now, the process of opening an account on the exchange platforms all you need to do before purchasing ETH. Let us look at some of the exchanges that are well known for opening accounts.

CEX.IO

You can visit CEX.io which is an exchange that allows the use of credit cards in the purchase of Ether and Bitcoin. It has high margin trading and other features common to other exchanges like selling cryptos directly to other people through their website and they also convert coins to fiat money.

- CEX is a major player in this field, and it has become an established exchange platform.
- CEX platform is easy to use, and it has great customer services. Even though it is a great platform, one of its drawbacks is the 48hours that non-US use shaves to wait for the verification process to complete.

Coinbase

This is the most popular exchange in the market today. It allows credit card purchase of Ethernet through their website. Coinbase also offers other services just like CEX does. Try it out. Coinbase is easy to use, and it has a minimalist layout. On the flip side, it is often down because of maintenance issues and slow customer relations.

Why do different exchanges have different prices?

The answer is quite simple. The prices differ for the same reason milk prices at different supermarkets. Each platform of the exchanges places their markup that results in a higher and lower price for the crypto assets.

It is recommended that you make a comparison between the exchanges you are going to consider to use in the purchase of Ethereum. The price differences may be insignificant, but let's get to it.

The price may be insignificant to you if you are purchasing to hold, but if you will be trading it on a regular basis and you have dived into the crypto business for a long time, then you will have to consider the price differences in the exchanges.

How to purchase Ethereum using Bitcoins

It is very easy to use Bitcoins to purchase Ether. The reason why we say this is because the verification process is already complete because the network already has confirmed that you are a legitimate customer, even though there are different ways Bitcoin can be bought anonymously, with small amounts.

Since you had been verified during the BTC purchase, opening an ETH wallet and selecting the cheaper exchange to convert your Bitcoin is the only step left. There is no need to look far for these options, CEX and Coinbase allow this type of transaction.

Poloniex

This is a great place to purchasing kind of altcoin. The platform offers insights in the cryptocurrency field, and it has tools that can analyze and trade all sorts of coins. You can buy Ethereum and any other major coins through this site with ease and explore the features of margin trading that are offered on this site. The drawback of Poloniex is the slow customer service.

GDAX

This is the brother of Coinbase. Coinbase is used mostly for the purchase, sale, and storage of Ethereum and other altcoins. But GDAX is used by pro traders who use digital assets to speculate. It is a stable platform that Ethereum and BTC are easily purchased. The tools for trading are available on this site.

Kraken Bitcoin Exchange

Kraken has been reviewed as a dependable exchange that users can use to purchase Ethereum. It does not have a confusing layout. However, it has a confusing and not so clear layout. If you get used to it, it gets easier to use, but it is not user-friendly. The best thing about it is its reliability in the purchase and trading of cryptos. On the drawback side, it takes time to understand the interface and the customer service card take time to offer support services.

How to store Ethereum Safely

Purchasing Ether is one side of the coin, the other sides its storage. It sounds straightforward and, but it is important to be serious about it because one might end up losing the coins that have been hard to get.

Ethereum storage

The best place that cryptocurrencies are kept is in the e-wallets, their wallets can serve as your bank account. You keep funds in the e-wallet, and it is the same place where you will receive and spend your coins.

There are quite some wallets that exist, and they all have distinct security levels.

We are going to have a quick summary:
Paper wallets are the most secure, followed by hardware wallets, desktop wallets, and hot wallets.

Ethereum Paper Wallets

Ethereum is stored securely using paper wallets. Paper wallets are private keys printed on a paper and placed in a safe. Several copies can be made that are stored in different locations. The greatest inconvenience is the trade-off that stands between the security and accessibility of paper wallets. Paper wallets are normally used in investments that are for the long term, and not for regular use.

Hardware Wallets

The hardware wallet option also offers high security because of its disconnection from the computer. These hardware devices are simply hardware devices that are used to place private keys of Ether at a safe pace. Since they cannot be accessed through a network, it is impossible to hack them. They have become popular when users are storing large amounts of tokens.

Trezor Hardware Wallet

It is one of the common hardware wallets in the market. It is used just the same way Ledger Nano S is used. It has a sleek look, and even though it has small buttons, it is still easy to use. The cheapest version retails at 89 Euros. Trezor is easy to use, supports altcoins and provides maximum security, but it is expensive.

Ledge Nano S

This is a hardware wallet that is used for the storage of Ethereum, Bitcoins, and other cryptos. It is extremely secure. The cheapest ledger retails at 69 Euros. If the cryptocurrency world is your playground, then you need to have it for the long term. The best thing about it is its high security and altcoin support. It is also easy to use, and the customer care support is great.

KeepKey Hardware Wallet

This hardware wallet is designed as a cold wallet to store Ethereum and other altcoins. It has a fancy design that is good for people who love nice looking gadgets. It retails at around $100. The best part about it is its high security, sleek design and how it supports all altcoins. The drawback is that its cheapest variant is costly when you compare it with Trezor or Nano S.

Summary

You are now informed about the places where you can buy and store Ethereum in a secure way. Ensure that you open an account on any exchange platform like CEX or Coinbase. The verification process should be done on the account after ID submission and a utility bill copy are submitted. Ethereum is then purchased directly using the credit card. Some Ethereum wallets are opened and distributed among them for risk dilution.

Buy a hardware wallet in case you will be keeping large amounts of coins for a long time. Don't store digital cash on mobile based hot wallets. Finally, in case you want to change to a particular fiat currency, sell the coins via the exchanges.

Chapter 10: How to Trade Ethereum

Trading is one profession that a trader has to prepare accordingly. A fact that needs to sink to anyone who wants to get into trading is that timing the buys and sells is a dream that should be left in wonderland. The probability of picking the top or the bottom is very hard if you combine it with the capital needed when trading, which if you lose after a bad trade, can dent your financial health. Trading is different in every way because each trader has different goals and this makes it hard to come up with a single way that someone can say is the true way of trading.

It is tough keeping yourself together after a series of bad trades. It is even hard for most traders to survive in the long run because of the psychological repercussions that traders experience. The best way traders should carry their daily practice is to forget about the past and focus on the present-day trading opportunities. You know, if you look at the past, one might think that getting into Bitcoin a year ago when the price was at $600 would have been a great investment with the amount of money one would be having right now. But sadly, that is not how it works. For instance, if you bought Bitcoin for $1,000 in 2013, then panicked when it fell to $200 and sold? The hindsight right now would be very painful. We can never correctly predict the future, it's all a fallacy. The best thing we can do I to learn from the past, and apply the lessons to the future decisions. Below are some tips for investors who would like to start trading cryptocurrencies.

The power that is in cryptocurrency

Cryptocurrencies like Bitcoin and Ethereum are not stocks; they are commodities. They are different but still have a process. The only similarity that exists between the two is the use of the exchange.

Cryptocurrency trading strategy

How many times will you make a buy or sell order? Many people try to engage in day trading, but it has been proven that holding the trade is the best way to do it. When trading, looking at the longer time will help you reduce the risk that you may incur, even there are times when you need to cut your losses and look for other opportunities.

We talked about diversifying our investment; we shall also look at how to diversify our capital when trading Ethereum and other altcoins. There is a term in crypto trading that is called *altcoin flipping*. It is known to be a rewarding way of making money online. We have already seen how accounts are created on cryptocurrency exchange platforms. Once you have funded the account, we are going to look at some useful ways of making profits out of trading Ethereum and other altcoins.

Divide your capital into different lot sizes for trading

I ensure that your capital is divided into five parts that are all equal. For instance, if you have 10 Bitcoins, then you will have to divide them into 2 Bitcoins per lot. The strategy uses 4 different lots to purchase different coins, leaving the fifth option for good entries that might emerge in the near future. For instance, a capital of 100 BTC is divided into 20 trading lots as below:

A) 20 BTC will be used to purchase Ethereum ETH
B) 20 BTC would be used to purchase Monero XMR

C) 20 BTC would be used to purchase Ethereum Classic ETC

D) 20 BTC would be used to purchase ripple XRP

Trading coins

One major benefit of cryptocurrencies is that it does not matter what the size of the capital is, coin's price that is suitable for you will always be able for you to make profits. But keep in mind that the capital size will determine the coins that can be profitable. For instance, if the worth of your capital is 20 BTC, it won't make any sense if you traded Ethereum while its price stands at 8BTC. This is because you will only have 2.5 coins of Ethereum with your capital. If you have a capital worth between 0.1 BTC - 0.2 BTC, it would be right if coins below 100,000 Satoshis are used. We are going to look at a portfolio that is worth 4 BTC, using a fictional altcoin price.

- 0.8 BTC for the purchase of Ethereum (0.0812 BTC=ETH)
- 0.8 BTC for the purchase of Ethereum classic (0.0044 BTC=ETC)
- 0.8 BTC for the purchase of monero (0.034 BTC=XMR)
- 0.8 BTC for the purchase of factom (0.0112 FCT)

- 0.8 BTC is left untouched for an upcoming trading opportunity.

In case you are in for a risky approach, you can use the fifth lot to buy cheaper coins that are valued less than 50,000 Satoshis. You can purchase Dogecoin, Bitshares, Steem, Synereo, Ripple, and many more. Ensure that you pick good coins for the flipping, dependent on the following factors.

Coins that have been introduced to Poloniex

We are going to use Poloniex as the exchange of choice for our case study. When the market of coins is open on Poloniex, high volumes that are volatile are experienced when the market is being established. New coins normally bring in the sense of profitability, especially if your timing of getting in and getting out is correct. January last year, PASC or Pascal Coin was introduced in the list of coins in Poloniex, and several people profited highly in two days.

Even though the market openings are profitable, they are normally followed by high volatility levels. You need to know the times to buy or sell. Volatility levels normally happen in the first weeks after the market opening. After the period, price stabilizes, and the coin's value withstands.

Poloniex Trading Volume

It is important to keep an eye on the Poloniex trading volume, since high trading volume coins represent profitable opportunities, especially if one knows when to buy or sell. On the Poloniex exchange's web page, a table with coins available for trading with volume of their day trading, and 24 hr price change percentage. When you press on the 'volume' column, you will be presented with a list of cons which will be arranged depending on the 24-hour trading volume, in a descending format.

News

News related to cryptocurrency is crucial when picking profitable coins. Crypto news needs to be followed through on a consistent basis. Below are some of the news sources you can be looking into.

A) You can log onto coindesk.com, Deepdotweb.com and much more

B) You can get to Bitcointalk.org to get promising ICOs and altcoins that are about to be launched

C) Coverage of news that is related to Ethereum and the whole concept of cryptocurrency. This is important because it allows one to follow the price volatility.

News has immense power on how cryptos are traded on a daily basis. Let us look at an example. Last year in February, Microsoft, Intel, JPMorgan, and other companies announced that they would be developing the use of Ethereum's blockchain in enterprises. This made a bullish rally kick off that led to a price increment of almost 100%. Traders who took advantage of the news profited in the bullish move.

The adoption of coins in Darknets and on Tor

Tor's marketplaces have the platforms used by cryptocurrencies, rather than speculative instruments and investment assets. Adoptions by new markets of crypts can soar prices. For instance, the adoption of deep web marketplaces like Oasis and Alphabay, took Monero as the payment method earlier this year. This led to the price of Monero to a value of $24.9.

Entry and exit places

Even though technical analysis does not work well with most cryptos due to the trading volumes that are low, there are signals that can be useful in getting good entries and exits. There are people who buy in the low, hold for a couple of days and then sell it for a profit. Below is the chart of a one-day timeframe of the GRCBTC from Poloniex.

Note: when you are looking at the charts in a technical analysis point of view, use Tradingview.com, because you can use oscillators and indicators in it. Any coin can be viewed on Poloniex.

We are going to look at the kinds of chart analysis and technical analysis of flipping any altcoins.

1. Use Tradeview.com for your chart viewing, because they can plot Fibonacci retracements, moving averages, and etc.
2. Ensure that you use Fibonacci retracements when you can. Plot your retracements from low to high on the 1-day timeframe within 4 months. You will realize great entry and exit points. In practice, something like this should be done.

Click on the 4-horizontal line icon on the tool's list that is located in the left part of the page, as shown below. You will see options will be present, click on the option of "Fib Retracement." Using your mouse, click on the 2 chart points, which represent the low and high of the fib retracement.

Price variation exploitation in different exchanges

It is better to set accounts of trading in different crypto exchanges. The following exchanges can be used in creating multiple accounts. HitBTC, Bittrex, and Poloniex. There are times when price varies minimally in exchanges before equilibrium is met. There are times when you can find a low buy of Dogecoin in Poloniex and sell it on HitBTC for a high price.

Chapter 11: The Future of Ethereum

As per experts, it is believed that Ethereum is here to for the long run. This is because of its infrastructure applications that make it possible to be used in diverse avenues.

There is a guarantee of other types of cryptocurrencies arising in the future that might be better than Ethereum. There is room for more tokens or coins in the near future.

With the enticement of making fast cash using token sales, others are likely to make a lot of money from them while others will bear the brunt of being ripped off. The likelihood of market manipulation in initial coin offerings occurring is high in the beginning, it is therefore important for you to know what you are getting into before being a victim of a fraud scheme.

Two out of four stages of Ethereum have occurred, these are:

- Frontier phase- which is the stage that everyone got when Ethereum was launched, and
- Homestead phase - which is where we are at the moment.

The other two upcoming stages are:

1. Metropolis phase - which has four main areas that are to be implemented;
   - Implementing various EIPs (Ethereum Improvement Protocols) that will help make Ethereum robust.
   - Flexibility towards smart contracts as they will pay their fees without the help of user funding.
   - Introduction of Zk-Snarks
   - Abstractions initial steps. This is to make Ethereum more "masses-friendly."

2. Serenity phase which is the last phase. Once it is launched:
   - More EIPs will be implemented
   - Changing from proof-of-work to proof-of-stake.
   - Abstraction of Ethereum will be complete.
   - Blockchain sharding will be implemented.

The future of transaction fees will be easier for the consumer. Fee companies, such as Mastercard or Visa charge a hefty fee once you make purchases with your credit card. With Ethereum, it will force companies to make a move to better cost handling of such transactions. Though there are some experts who do not think that banks will modify their price models very easily.

There are some banks that are interested in incorporating blockchains, Bitcoin, and the like into their systems. The only law they want to remain is that of "know your customer", to which they want to be obeyed. It will help eradicate geographic incumbents but be hubs for the new means of financing businesses. Rules will make the transition smoother, until then it is important to be transparent on what one is doing.

It is likely that the prices will stabilize in the future. To achieve this, they can have a use-case which trumps traditional money. Interactions with various people around the world will require an international currency that is acceptable, not everyone has a dollar bill. The process of acquiring such a currency might take some time, but the need to have transactions beyond one's borders will increase.

Ethereum and other ICOs are changing the way entrepreneurs seek funds. The way to do this is by telling as many people who are interested in the business and want to participate to contribute.

In the long run, Ethereum wants to "disappear." This is a term used to mean that it will be part of our daily lives that people will be using it or working on something that is related to Ethereum. It is a long way from happening, before it is implemented everywhere and into everything that can use ether; yet the future does look bright for Ethereum.

Conclusion

Thank for making it through to the end of Ethereum, let's hope it was informative and able to provide you with all of the tools you need to understand this revolutionary technology. Just because you've finished this book doesn't mean there is nothing left to learn on the topic, expanding your horizons is the only way to find the mastery you seek.

The next step is to stop reading and to get starting doing whatever it is that you need to do to either prepare yourself for the future, or invest in Ethereum, or better yet, trade it over time. If you find that you are interested in DApp, you will need further studies in learning more about programming in Ethereum. Start off by researching the right books and make a schedule of how you are going to track your lessons until you can code DApps.

Studies show that complex tasks that are broken down into individual pieces, including individual deadlines, have a much greater chance of being completed when compared to something that has a general need of being completed but no real timetable for doing so. Even if it seems silly, go ahead and set your own deadlines for completion, complete with indicators of success and failure. After you have completed all of your required preparations, you will be glad you did. You will be able to write your DApps and learn more about Ethereum and blockchain.

Once you have identified your field of interest regarding Ethereum, it is important that you understand what it truly entails. The future of blockchain is bright, and you never know when the perfect opportunity may arise. When you use the knowledge you have acquired to prepare for this innovation, you will feel that you have taken a step in a growing field that has great potential.

Finally, if you found this book useful in any way, a review on Amazon is always appreciated!

Free Bonus!

Grab your free copy of the cryptocurrency research toolkit.

When I first started off researching for cryptocurrency I did not know where to do my research. Type in the link below to enjoy where I do my own research before investing in any coin.

http://bit.ly/cryptoresearch

www.ingramcontent.com/pod-product-compliance
Lightning Source LLC
Chambersburg PA
CBHW031447210526
45464CB00005B/2363